Treasure Basket
Explorations
Heuristic Learning
for Infants and Toddlers

Laura Wilhelm, EdD

Gryphon House
www.gryphonhouse.com

Treasure Basket
Explorations
Heuristic Learning
for Infants and Toddlers

Laura Wilhelm, EdD

Copyright

Published by Gryphon House, Inc.
P. O. Box 10, Lewisville, NC 27023
800.638.0928; 877.638.7576 (fax)
Visit us on the web at www.gryphonhouse.com.

Cover photograph courtesy of Shutterstock.
Photography by Bree Hines, Stacey Hines, Goldie Thompson, Kathryn Riley, Hope Wiggs, Ginger Welch, and Laura Wilhelm. Some interior photographs used under license from Shutterstock.com.

Library of Congress Cataloging-in-Publication Data
The Cataloging-in-Publication data is registered with the Library of Congress for 978-0-87659-575-6.

Bulk Purchase

Gryphon House books are available for special premiums and sales promotions as well as for fund-raising use. Special editions or book excerpts also can be created to specifications. For details, call 800.638.0928.

Disclaimer

Gryphon House, Inc., cannot be held responsible for damage, mishap, or injury incurred during the use of or because of activities in this book. Appropriate and reasonable caution and adult supervision of children involved in activities and corresponding to the age and capability of each child involved are recommended at all times. Do not leave children unattended at any time. Observe safety and caution at all times.

Table of Contents

Dedication

Dedicated to the babies and toddlers who patiently teach us—and to all the grown-ups who listen.

Acknowledgments

Special thanks to Carolyn Lamiell and her enthusiastic team at Southern Hills Child Development Center, as well as to Dianna Ross, Margaret Napier, and the rest of the wonderfully helpful people at the Cleo L. Craig Child Development Laboratory at Oklahoma State University. This book is possible because you welcomed us into your world!

An enormous thank you to all the beautiful children who appear in this book (and to those who don't) for sharing a glimpse into the serious business of learning.

And thank you to the wonderful folks behind the cameras: Hope Wiggs, Kathryn Riley, Stacey Hines, Bree Hines, Goldie Thompson, and Ginger Welch.

Introduction

Treasure baskets and heuristic play were conceived by Elinor Goldschmied, a pioneer of early care and education in the United Kingdom, Italy, and Spain. In her 1994 book, *People under Three*, she and coauthor Sonia Jackson assert that babies and toddlers deserve as much respect as adults give one another. They knew, as many parents and grandparents know, that babies often prefer to play with ordinary objects such as kitchen utensils and even the box a toy came in rather than the commercially made toy itself. A treasure basket filled with ordinary items can be endlessly fascinating to a young child.

Goldschmied envisioned treasure baskets as a special activity reserved for children during that short period of life when they are able to sit comfortably but are not yet mobile. For children who are walking through age three, she adapted to their newfound mobility and drive to explore by developing a related approach: heuristic play. The term *heuristic* refers to discovery by a trial-and-error method. Because a child who has learned to walk will rarely be content to remain seated at a basket, heuristic-play sessions begin with the family member or teacher setting up small collections of interesting materials around a room. The children then have time and freedom to explore the new treasures.

Goldschmied believed that the youngest children, once thought of as helpless creatures, are actually amazingly capable people. For anyone who takes the time to watch, her approach showcases a child's capabilities. Observing treasure baskets and heuristic play gives adults opportunities to see children use trial and error, which makes their thinking visible. Rather than defining infant and toddler classrooms in terms of things the babies can't do—play on the preschool playground, paint in the art room, or eat lunch with the other classes—we can see what these people, so new to the planet, have already figured out and are in the process of determining. Use this book to inspire incorporation of open-ended explorations into your infant and toddler program. The children will benefit, and so will you!

Creating a Space for Exploration

All beautiful things encourage a child's sense of wonder,
and everything that encourages a child's sense of
wonder is beautiful.

—Mitsumasa Anno, Japanese illustrator and children's author

Babies joyfully move their own bodies and interact with adults during the first few months of life. This is all the entertainment they need. Then, around three months of age, babies' hands become their first toys. Accidentally at first, then intentionally, they are able to swipe, grasp, and move objects by themselves. A new sense of wonder and

excitement about the big wide world frames their first big question: "What is this?" To find an answer, babies explore in every way they can: looking, moving the thing with their arms, hands, or feet, and ultimately bringing it to their mouths to be gnawed on. Gumming gives the baby more information about the object—how it tastes, how it smells, and how it reacts to the pressure of being gummed. It may also bring relief to tender gums about to sprout new teeth. This stage of new discovery is the perfect time to introduce treasure baskets.

Infant-toddler classrooms are often arranged for adult convenience and to comply with safety regulations. Even homes tend to fill up with "things to put babies in," including cradles, carriers, bouncers, swings, high chairs, play seats, propping pillows, and strollers. A baby who is strapped in is not free to move his body and explore his surroundings.

Providing a treasure basket and the time to explore it will create opportunities to capture a baby's interest when he is calm but also actively engaged and curious. The watchful adult following the baby's interests can help him form secure attachments.

Psychologist George Forman, coeditor of *The Hundred Languages of Children*, believes in the power of ordinary moments in infant and toddler classrooms. He asks teachers to wear small video cameras to capture everyday interactions, which he then uses to illustrate important concepts of child development. Treasure baskets and heuristic play can help us notice the same powerful moments.

For children who are not yet walking, arrange items attractively into baskets that the children can sit beside and explore at their own pace. For toddlers, create islands of discovery by putting out piles of the items, as well as purses, cardboard boxes, and cracker or cookie tins that the children can put the objects in, take them out of, and create their own games with. Think of these activities as another way to have center time or free play.

Babies are amazing. Researchers once thought they were helpless creatures with undeveloped senses and even debated their ability to feel pain. Now we know that newborns not only feel pain, but they can also recognize their own mother's milk by smell and can recognize their parent's voices from their first day! Spending time in the company of babies presents opportunities to get to know each child's personality. The items selected for the treasure basket can add to meaningful

curriculum and can be tailored to meet the goals of any program, classroom, and school. Teachers and family members can brainstorm together, sharing observations about innovative ways that the items are being used by children and the wonderful ideas that children are testing.

Child care providers have tremendous potential to strengthen families. Teachers who communicate stories of what a child does in class each day can paint family members a picture of the child's achievements and emerging personality during the hours that family members miss. As pediatrician and author T. Berry Brazelton has shown us through his book and video series *Touchpoints*, newborns can track a red ball with their eyes, imitate tongue thrusts, and turn their heads toward familiar voices on the day they are born. Each subsequent day of life, infants are building and strengthening concepts of their world by experiencing ordinary moments of exploration.

What Is a Treasure Basket?

A treasure basket is a sturdy, open basket piled with a variety of everyday objects. Placed where babies can reach it, the basket allows babies to choose what they want to explore. A treasure basket should include a variety of textures, such as loofah sponges, wooden spoons, and shiny tin boxes. It should include objects that a child can place inside another object and then dump out again. The collected materials should appeal to a child's senses. Some good options could be made of metal; be organic, such as pinecones or seashells; or be made of fabric, such as wide lengths of ribbon or fuzzy or coarse material. Such objects provide an opportunity to create different sounds by dropping or banging them together.

Treasure baskets can be introduced as soon as a child can sit up on his own, usually at about five or six months. Use the baskets as long as

His caregiver observed a four-month-old lifting, shaking, and dropping a cotton handkerchief and gazing at its interesting pattern as the baby lay on a blanket spread on the floor. The child's exploration of the handkerchief lasted for sixteen minutes.

a child is interested, but most children will lose interest as soon as they are able to walk. The freedom of mobility brings an irresistible restlessness. Children who can walk are seldom content to remain seated at a basket, so teachers and family members often move on to the movement-friendly activity of heuristic play.

What Makes Treasure Baskets Special?

Treasure baskets are a meaningful approach to teaching and learning, because the focus of the lesson is on observing the child. The adult observer should look for answers to questions such as, "What is this child capable of at this moment in time?" "What has changed since my last opportunity to watch this baby explore the objects in the treasure basket?" "What can I learn about his intellectual, physical, and social development just by watching him explore these ordinary and unremarkable, yet intriguing, materials?" Treasure baskets give caregivers a chance to notice each child's interests. Because the main adult activity is observation, it can be a chance to relax for a moment during an otherwise hectic day. The activities of the child take center stage. The adult role is to talk less, watch, and learn from the child.

In the first years of life, four compelling questions guide children's learning:

- What is this?
- What can I do with it?
- What else can this do?
- What can this become?

Between three and six months of age, children notice objects in their immediate surroundings. The first big question, "What is this?" drives children to gaze, vocalize, and move their hands or arms toward faces, pets, and objects in an attempt to learn more about them. From about five to twelve months, children are able to grasp, manipulate, and mouth objects. They are able to take in information through their five senses to learn more about the thing, which leads them to the second big question: "What can I do with it?"

As children begin to master their world by crawling and walking where they want to go, they gain access to much more of the environment. Between twelve and twenty-four months, their new skills lead to the third big question: "What else can this do?" As toddlers enter their third year of life, between twenty-

You can almost see the wheels turning in a toddler's mind as he tries to enclose a string of pearly beads in a brightly flowered cosmetics bag. He notices extra room in the bag and tries to fill the space with more beads. But then the bag won't zip, so he removes some beads. This time he's successful in zipping it closed but notices that there's an empty space again, so he starts over. His caregiver observed this two-year-old persist at this problem for half an hour.

four and thirty-six months, they start to incorporate more language into their play. The fourth big question, "What can this become?" ushers in a new era of pretending. Small toys become play food as children imitate adults cooking. Baby dolls are cared for, and anything from a shoe to a block becomes a car.

Before children can sit up, they may enjoy grasping items. From three months of age, children may enjoy having two or three interesting objects to look at and grasp. Cotton handkerchiefs with an interesting pattern or a lace edge are easy for the baby to move and won't smack him in the head the way a rattle can. As babies begin to master the movements of their fingers, they may like exploring items that can be easily grasped, such as silicone kitchen tools, wicker balls, and rolled-up socks.

Sitting up gives a six-month-old child an entirely new view of the world. He can now sit well enough not to rely on his arms for balance. This gives him the freedom to grasp objects he sees and bring them to his mouth. From the time a baby can sit comfortably without needing his hands for support, he is ready for a treasure basket.

The basket should have sides sturdy enough to help support him. It should not have a handle to get in his way as he selects items to grasp, mouth, gnaw, and drop. Provide a treasure basket that is low enough so that the child can easily reach in to retrieve objects and sturdy enough not to flip if the baby leans an elbow on the rim. Some people will even spread a white sheet under a basket to reduce the distraction of brightly colored carpets and make it easier for a baby to spot and retrieve dropped items.

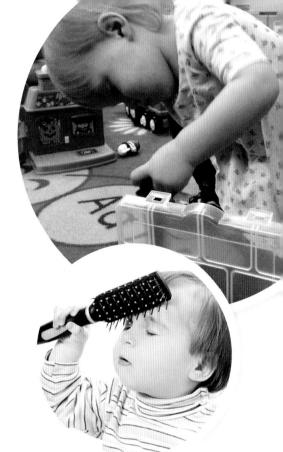

When a child begins walking, heuristic play through islands of discovery is designed to capture both the child's interest and to honor his need to move around the room. Setting up the classroom with small islands of intriguing objects invites the child to move around the room to explore, but giving a classroom full of toddlers the freedom to explore piles of new things might be a frightening proposition. Children actually become calmer and more focused during heuristic play. Some schools around the United States and internationally have even decided to use only heuristic materials and to get rid of plastic toys altogether.

How to Create and Introduce Treasure Baskets

> Be careful what you teach. It might interfere
> with what they are learning.
>
> —Magda Gerber, founder of Resources for Infant Educarers

Start with a sturdy basket about 6" x 18", without a handle if possible. Handles make the basket harder to tip over but may also get in a child's way, preventing her from reaching something she's after. Inside the basket, place a variety of items. Look for safe, beautiful, well-made items that appeal to the senses. Each treasure basket can be unique and customized for each child's or group's interests.

Once you've made a treasure basket, invite friends to help find items to make more. You can find treasures at thrift stores and garage sales, and they can be donated by families at your school. Just make sure the items are sturdy enough to hold up to daily sanitizing.

What to Include and Why

Treasure baskets should continually evolve as your inspiration and children's interests change. Let your senses be your guide when selecting materials. A well-stocked treasure basket should be so inviting that you want to play with it yourself. Begin with visual variety. Even natural surfaces will have a variety of shades. Include larger items such as loofah sponges and smaller items such as the tin boxes for mints. Empty boxes from Valentine's Day chocolates are beautiful and smell yummy. They may have liners that make great noises in a baby's hands, even though the paper doesn't last long. Children are fascinated with unusual textures, such as pinecones, large seashells, and spiky hair curlers. They also love the surprising sounds that things make when dropped or banged together. A ring of measuring spoons makes a great instrument, and wooden spoons can turn anything into a drum. Chapter 3 lists a number of categories and items to get you started. Of course safety is the primary consideration.

Avoid using plastic items in a treasure basket. Although plastic comes in different shapes and colors, it tends to feel, smell, and taste the same regardless of shape or color. It also doesn't absorb body heat the way metal items can. Changes in temperature can add to a child's experience.

If you are concerned about the safety of an object, simply choose something else. Although plastics should generally be avoided, some plastic items can be really interesting. Consider including a TV remote (without the batteries and with any tiny screws secured with a drop of super glue) or silicone kitchen gadgets. Eliminate choking hazards by making sure items and their parts cannot fit completely inside a choke-tube tester, available from several school-supply companies. If items become chipped, ripped, or broken, remove them. Be sure to inspect the items after each use, and have regularly scheduled times to inspect and refresh the objects

you include. Make sure items are clean with no loose parts or parts that may become loose during play.

Collect items for your own treasure baskets. Unless just one child is awake while the others are napping, infants and toddlers are almost always interested in being where the action is. Create multiple treasure baskets with this in mind. Include multiples of the most intriguing items, because conflicting interests may be inevitable.

There are many sources for items to include in treasure baskets. For example, ZeroLandfill is an upcycling project that began in 2006. Architectural and interior design firms and contractors donate their unused, outdated, or leftover tiles, carpet samples, and wallpaper to a central location where the public can choose any of the materials they would like to take. There is no charge to collect materials. Local manufacturers and retailers are also potential sources for interesting castoffs.

Initially, present each child with her own basket, but don't be surprised if other children choose to join in the fun around a particular basket for extended play. They will eventually notice and then branch out to explore the other baskets in the room. Of course, some children will lose interest sooner than others. Have several sturdy books or blocks ready to help children transition to the next activity in the daily plan.

Introducing Treasure Baskets

For most child care centers, the transition to incorporating treasure baskets and heuristic play will be gradual. Introduce a few treasure baskets into an infant classroom, and notice how the babies respond. Or, set up heuristic materials for toddlers on a rainy day. Then conduct a staff-development session to explain the approach. Ask teachers who have used the activities to share their firsthand observations. Invite all of the teachers to share worries and concerns, and brainstorm ways to address concerns. If the staff members are interested in expanding the approach, host a family meeting to explain why you will begin implementing treasure baskets and heuristic play. Enlist family members to help gather additional materials and develop ways to organize and store them. Teacher or family member volunteers can sign up to inspect and replace items as needed.

Offer treasure baskets as a regular but distinct part of the children's daily or weekly routine.

Find an appropriate time in the schedule to try introducing treasure baskets; successful implementation may be a matter of timing. Consider, for example, offering treasure baskets first thing in the morning to help children transition away from their families. Some teachers expect a calmer classroom mid-morning when many children are likely to be comfortably settled in and alert, so they choose to introduce treasure baskets at those times. Others like to introduce something new in smaller increments as children begin to wake from afternoon naps. Decide what might work best in your schedule.

Treasure baskets are mobile by their very nature, so they can easily be taken outdoors. When children lose interest in the baskets, they can wander freely to other available outdoor activities. Baskets can also be easily set up in hallways or gym spaces to give little ones a change of scenery on inclement-weather days.

Thirty minutes to an hour should provide ample time for meaningful explorations and cleanup. Cleaning up can become an extension of play because returning the objects to the basket can be as much fun as playing with them, especially if the items rattle or produce a satisfying *thunk* as they land. Cleanup time can be an important component of the lesson plan.

As children explore the baskets, follow their lead and use supportive body language and interested facial expressions, but try not to dominate or direct what the child is doing. The idea is to step back and observe. Watching, writing details in a notebook, or recording video can provide you with authentic learning stories to share with other teachers and family members, as well as documentation to revisit over time. An electronic tablet or phone with recording capability can provide an opportunity for practitioners and even the child to instantly see what they were just doing. Technology offers a new way to reflect. After observing herself on video, the child may choose to repeat an action or try something new.

Implementing Heuristic Play

Like treasure baskets, islands of discovery are not a new curriculum but an activity as old as play itself. Heuristic play can work into existing curriculum as a special activity hour during the day or week. Begin by gathering materials—lots of materials—but don't put everything out at once. A fifteen-inch milk crate–type cart can hold all of the materials needed for a class of twelve to fifteen children. For larger or combined classes, a few of the crates work perfectly. Put a few items out in the classroom, and keep extras ready in the hall or on a shelf. As you see which items are popular that day, add more of those.

Set out heuristic materials in small piles around the classroom. You can do this while children are out of the room eating, playing outdoors, napping, or just taking a walk around the hallways. When they return to the classroom, they will find it transformed: a  small mound of scarves and neckties in one corner, some pans and measuring cups and spoons in another. A small rug is a good spot to place seashells and pinecones. A mug tree decorated with bracelets and napkin rings makes an excellent game for practicing eye-hand coordination. Place several containers such as purses, bags, buckets, and boxes near each pile. Children at this age love to gather, collect, and distribute. It is important to remember that when a child hands her treasures to another child, this isn't really sharing yet, and she may be back to collect "her" things.

Some teachers like to drape covers over the shelves containing the regular classroom blocks and toys during island time, so the environment conveys a message that this is a special time during which unique items are available for deliberate, unhurried examination.

Playing It Safe

As with all activities involving young children, weigh the risks and benefits. If a material seems unsafe, replace it with a safer alternative. A watchful adult nearby will make any activity safer. Some of the suggested materials may not be safe for a particular child. Caregivers must make judgement calls, decide which materials are likely to be safe, and then supervise their use. Remove anything that children use unsafely.

Children under the age of four should not be given objects less than 1 1/4" x 2 1/4". Smaller objects can cause children to choke. Young children are especially at risk for choking, because they explore so many things with their mouths. They are still developing motor skills and

may not be able to indicate that they are choking. This is another reason for close supervision.

Unfinished, untreated wooden items work well because they don't have potentially unsafe varnish or paint. If you are unsure about lead or other chemicals in a material, seal the items inside a plastic bottle with a secured lid. The children can explore the translucence of the container and the sound of the items while not touching or mouthing them.

More information about protecting young children from lead and other environmental hazards is available through the Environmental Protection Agency at https://www.epa.gov/lead and the Centers for Disease Control and Prevention at https://www.cdc.gov/nceh/lead/tips/ sources.htm.

Examine materials each time they are brought out and put away. Look for chips, cracks, and breaks. Each center should have a specific person assigned to regularly examine and update the materials. Damaged items should be removed to be repaired or discarded. Because young children explore with their mouths, materials should be sanitized after each use. Fabric can be washed in a washing machine. You can run other items through a dishwasher or spray them with a bleach-and-water solution and allow them to air dry.

Some schools store treasure baskets and containers with heuristic materials on shelves in a central closet for many classes to share. Open-top drawer organizers are useful for corralling items inside wheeled milk crates. Pillowcases or shoe bags hung on a row of coat hooks on the wall are also great places to store heuristic materials. Label the bags with what goes inside so older toddlers can help sort the items as they help clean up.

Treasure baskets work well with children who have special needs. These children are able to participate with their peers.

Using Language and Heuristic Play to Support Learning

> Wherever possible the adult acts as facilitator rather than director of the child's activities . . . in the context of a carefully planned and organized environment.
>
> —Sonia Jackson, *coauthor of* People under Three

C hildren learn through open-ended play and exploration. Attentive adults can support learning by encouraging the child's sense of independence and discovery. Present activities that are easy enough that they aren't frustrating but challenging enough that they aren't boring. There will be time for academics and formal instruction later. Children need opportunities to construct broad general concepts about the world before focusing on narrow skills.

We now know that early experiences affect how the brain is wired and set the stage for later behavior and social competence. Implementing treasure baskets and heuristic play within daily or weekly plans adds opportunities for joyful exploration. Attentive observation by adults strengthens secure attachment bonds for children. Time spent watching young children explore gives teachers opportunities to reflect on why they are passionate about teaching babies and toddlers. There is nothing quite like watching joy light up a child's face when he discovers something new as he plays. The concentration on little ones' faces as they try out new ideas conveys the seriousness with which they approach their world.

Play research shows that we do not need to choose between play and learning. Play is learning. Intentional teachers expand learning opportunities by supporting children's natural interests through play. The International Play Association's "Declaration of the Child's Right to Play" was developed for the International Year of the Child in 1979 and revised in 1989 in conjunction with the United Nations Convention on the Rights of the Child. It states that play is a basic need for children, vital to healthy development.

Programs such as the infant-toddler centers and preschools of Reggio Emilia, Italy, where adults reflect philosophically about children as they are today rather than the students and adults they will become, seek to inspire and honor children's creative ideas. Teachers and children are partners in the process of inviting novel ideas and sustaining learning. Children are encouraged to express themselves in "a hundred languages."

Heuristic play with familiar and natural materials also works beautifully outdoors as an informal curricular activity. Nature preschools are popping up around the world in response to overly academic and digitized trends in childhood. Nature and forest schools promote creativity and independence in outdoor or woodland settings, yet address the same goals as traditional preschools. According to Joseph Cornell, author of *Sharing Nature*, children who spend time in nature become calmer and more observant. Even *Sesame Street* has devoted time to nature and science, inspired by the nature preschool movement.

The wisdom and wonder of open-ended materials are confirmed through the expanding popularity of loose-parts play. Loose parts, such as blocks, scarves, and boxes, are materials that can be carried, constructed, stacked, lined up, fit together, balanced, and piled. According to architect Simon Nicholson, the loose parts in our environment inspire our creativity, and the more variables available, the more inventive humans will become. Playing with loose parts provides endless opportunities for young children to expand their thinking and test new ideas.

Treasure baskets and heuristic play are an approach, not a curriculum. They work well as an addition to many popular curriculum programs. Heuristic play and treasure baskets are designed as special activities to be brought out at a planned time each day or a few times a week. After forty-five minutes or an hour, as the children begin to lose interest, put the baskets away to bring them out again at another time. Materials can be stored in a central location and shared by several classrooms. Children find the materials exciting because they present fresh challenges each time they arrive.

Young children can focus their attention for about one minute per year of age. An almost magical aspect of treasure baskets is their ability to capture a child's attention for extended periods. Take note of which items children mouth, look at, try to mash into other objects, put down, return to, or bang on the floor. Also notice which items are briefly lifted and then discarded. Compare your observation notes over time. You will be amazed at the development of new ideas, motor skills, and behavior patterns that you have documented.

As a child builds memories and experiences, his preferences will change. Some children will imitate what others are doing or even bring objects to the attention of other children. Unhurried time to explore provides opportunity for social interaction among children. A treasure basket offered to one baby may result in four more crawling over to watch. Even when presented with their own individual baskets, some babies continue to be immersed in observing the first child.

Because these items are not commercially made toys, they present novel experiences. Babies will explore the items' properties using all of their senses. Surprisingly, eyeglass cases snap shut quite suddenly but do not

pinch little fingers. Metal kitchen whisks have an unfamiliar taste and perfectly finger-sized spaces between the springy wires. A ring of stainless steel measuring spoons will hit the ground with a satisfying crash. Spontaneity follows the initial startling surprise, and children will work diligently to create the unexpected action again.

The sensory nature of treasure baskets makes them uniquely suited for most children. You can create baskets filled with items that can be handled masterfully by each child in a particular class. Children with limited vision may enjoy the tactile and auditory variety of objects that you have selected for these qualities. Because treasure-basket exploration takes place in a defined space, children with physical and visual limitations will feel safe and secure as they investigate. Each treasure basket can be customized for children whose behaviors may indicate neurological differences, including those on the autism spectrum. Try providing calming, soothing experiences through materials such as weighty bean bags, squeezable sponges, and sealed containers of liquid. Each child will find his preferences and favorite items. Children with hearing impairments may enjoy the visual and tactile variety of a treasure basket or heuristic-play materials. Because the child's actions direct the play, he can repeat movements that cause vibrations in the objects.

Some people are surprised to find that babies already have their own personalities and ideas. The beauty of heuristic learning is that, by observing a very young child exploring objects that are new to him, family members and caregivers can start to notice and share stories about his preferences for particular things and how those preferences change from day to day. "Yesterday he couldn't get enough of the stainless-steel coaster. Today he's fascinated with a wooden spoon!" These conversations can help each person understand the child better and plan activities to build on his interests. Reserve time each day or week to watch carefully as a child follows his own ideas in heuristic play. You will begin to see the child as the person he is today, rather than pushing the child toward the future. Mindfulness will bring new respect for the child's wonderful ideas and will impart intentionality to your teaching.

100 Sensory Items to Put in a Treasure Basket or Island of Discovery

Treasure baskets and islands of discovery should appeal to the senses. Decide which of the items below will work best for the children in your care, then supervise closely. Sanitize each item after every use. Discard any items that become chipped, broken, or unsafe.

Items with Interesting Textures

- Natural loofah sponges

- Pinecones

- Small baskets

- Kitchen whisks

- Sponge hair curlers

- Velcro hair rollers

- Woven-loop potholders

- Crocheted potholders

- Lace

- Silicone kitchen funnels

- Giant pom-poms

- Crescent wrenches

- Lawn-sprinkler connectors

- Toolboxes with trays

- Mug trees to hang bracelets and napkin rings

- Silk ties

- Wool coin purse

- Leather wallet

- Old remote controls (batteries removed)

- Wicker paper-plate holders

- Wooden rolling pin

- Marble rolling pin

- Dishcloth

- Pumice stone

- Large sink stopper

Items that Make Interesting Noises

- Cookie tins
- Metal measuring spoons
- Metal measuring cups
- Wooden spoons
- Serving spoons
- Pots
- Pans
- Beads inside a plastic bottle
- Liners from valentine chocolate boxes
- Eyeglass cases
- PVC pipe in 12–18-inch sections
- Copper cookie cutters
- Large seashells
- Sand shovels
- Sand pails
- Spatulas
- Canning jars

- Slotted spoons
- Drumsticks
- Salad servers
- Bamboo tongs
- Brown paper
- Muffin tins
- Kitchen timer
- Bundt pan

Items that Look Beautiful

- Napkin rings

- Wide bracelets

- Railroad insulators

- Unbreakable mirrors

- Embroidered hankies

- Ribbon

- CDs or DVDs

- Coasters

- Tiles

- Silk scarves

- Paperweights

- Faux-fur earmuffs

- Wooden spools

- Purses

- Steamer baskets

- Wooden bowls

- Scrunchies

- Place mats

- Hotel key cards

- Big rocks

- Tree branches with bark

- Silk flowers

- Large bulldog clips

- Calendars

- Mugs

Items that Appeal to a Variety of Senses

- Empty breath-mint containers
- Valentine chocolate boxes
- Cardboard containers
- Smoothly sanded wood
- Metal spoons
- Velvet ribbons
- Copper gelatin molds
- Small cutting boards
- Potato mashers
- Tea strainers
- Oranges
- Lemons
- Grapefruit
- Makeup brushes
- Wide paintbrushes
- Paint rollers
- Bath poufs
- Empty tissue boxes

- Feather dusters
- Aluminum foil
- Waxed paper
- Denim
- Maracas
- Zippered cosmetic cases
- Keys

Tailoring Treasure Baskets to Specific Goals

> Senses other than sight can prove avenues of delight and discovery, storing up memories and impressions.
>
> —Rachel Carson, American marine biologist and conservationist

You may already be using some heuristic materials in your classroom. Many programs include strings of beads or necklaces, real dishes, pans, wooden spoons, large seashells, and smooth blocks of wood. Heuristic play is an opportunity to provide variety by bringing in fresh examples of these types of materials.

As they explore these materials, children will be developing eye-hand coordination and motor planning, testing their ideas, verbalizing, sharing ideas, and experimenting with cause and effect. The properties of each object—transparency, a shiny surface, a rough or slick texture—cause children to play with them longer as they try to make sense of unfamiliar properties.

Treasure Baskets and Developmental Milestones

Strengthening Muscles, Using the Eyes, and Responding to Sound

Babies are getting to know the people who love them, and they can tell us what we need to know about them. If we observe carefully, babies' behaviors will guide us to what they want and need. Gazing at a brightly colored scarf or a person's face shows they are interested.

Fussing or turning away means they are ready for a break. A mindful adult can read a baby's cues and respond in a way that builds the baby's confidence.

Between birth and three months, babies need tummy time— waking time spent on their stomachs during which they can strengthen their neck and shoulder muscles by lifting their heads and chests. Placing some shiny measuring cups and textured potholders nearby can capture a baby's gaze and maybe even elicit a fleeting smile. An empty container that will make noise when it tips over near a baby's feet presents an opportunity for the child to explore cause and effect as she stretches and kicks while on her back. Opening and shutting her hands provide the infant the possibility to grasp lightweight objects, which she will want to explore further by bringing her hands to her mouth. Babies show a strong preference for people. They will turn toward a person's voice, and they prefer familiar voices over those of strangers. They will mimic facial expressions and expect responses to their vocal sounds.

Sitting Up and Grasping Objects

As babies start to roll over, they can travel toward scattered treasures that interest them. Sitting up without the support of their hands and holding their heads steady gives them a whole new perspective. With their hands now freed, they can easily reach in and grasp treasures from the basket and can move them from hand to hand. They are now able to dig into the basket for partially hidden items and will struggle to grasp those items that are just out of reach. Babies may encourage interaction through smiles and moving their arms and legs, as well as by cooing, babbling, and making other sounds.

Moving and Exploring

As babies begin to scoot and crawl, they can chase after balls and cylinders that roll away from them. They can sit up on their own and pull upright on furniture to cruise along its edge. Stranger anxiety may begin at this age because they know trusted adults exist even when they cannot see them. Treasure baskets can be a comforting activity at drop-off time or can

be used to help ease anxiety with a new caregiver or classroom. At this age, we can observe preferences for favorite items, although the favorite selections change often. Babies will begin to imitate ways they've seen items used before, and they will find new ways to explore with all their senses. Babies this age are starting to understand what you say and can even follow some simple directions.

Walking and Discovering

Walking is a huge transformation in the life of a toddler. They will often be so consumed with walking and thinking about walking that they may lose their appetites and may even lose sleep. This is the perfect time to transition from treasure baskets, which are designed for the baby to be seated next to them, to islands of discovery. Islands of discovery are little piles of heuristic-play materials arranged around a classroom. This shift allows for the child's need to be in motion as she discovers the new materials placed throughout her environment. By this age, toddlers can say no and show a preference for independence.

Encourage children to talk about their discoveries and invent wonderful new uses for them. They may be able to say between fifty and one hundred words. They will often imitate what they've seen others do: using bowls and tubs as cooking pots and using remote controls as telephones. Provide plenty of items such as scarves and necklaces that the toddlers can bring to their friends. But, be ready to help them negotiate when they want those items returned; sharing is not a concept they understand yet.

Talking, Comparing, and Interacting

Two-year-olds are becoming much more social and will often play the same roles as those children who are nearby. They may use 900 words by their third birthday. This exploding language ability lets them label items and helps adults better understand what they are thinking. They will often multitask as they've seen adults do. A child may hold a phone to her ear while putting on a scarf and stirring a pot, for example. Children this age like to sort items, such as lining up pinecones by size or ordering rocks by color. They also like to fit things into boxes, purses, and bags, which they may use to transport more than it looks like they can carry, or they may surprise a friend with what's inside.

Heuristic play through treasure baskets and islands of discovery fits very well with Swiss psychologist Jean Piaget's ideas about a child's construction of knowledge. Piaget categorized learning into three types of knowledge: physical, logical-mathematical, and social.

- **Physical knowledge** is directly constructed by the child as she interacts with objects, noticing their shapes, colors, textures, and weights.

- **Logical-mathematical knowledge** is built by the child as she compares the properties of two or more objects. For example, she may explore and begin to understand that two balls are different in size (one is bigger than the other), but they are both round.

- **Social knowledge** requires interacting with others, and the child learns the language used in social conventions. Adults can support this learning through natural conversations, naming objects as the child explores them, and talking about how items are used in daily activities.

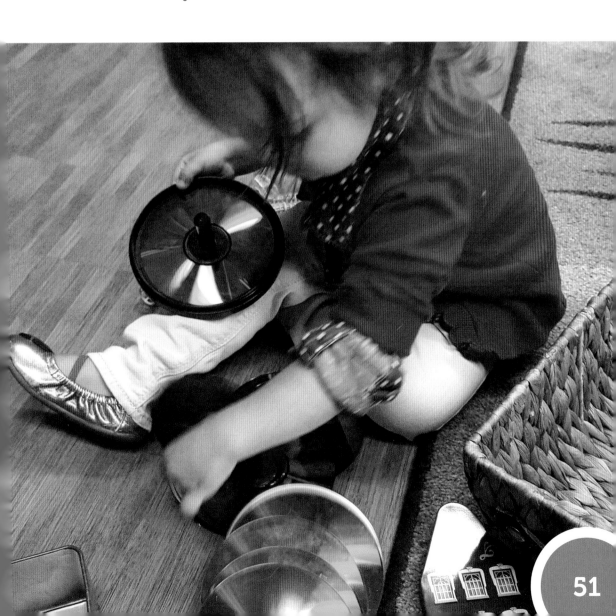

Treasure Baskets by Age

Stand aside for a while and leave room for learning,
observe carefully what children do, and then, if you have
understood well, perhaps teaching will be different
from before.

—Loris Malaguzzi, pioneer of the Reggio Emilia philosophy

C hildren's interests will develop and change as they grow. Pay close attention to the items that attract a child, and note when the child loses interest and moves on to other items.

Newborn to Five Months: What Is This?

For very young babies, newborn to five months, the objects that are likely to capture their attention are those that are easy for them to see, reach for, and, eventually, grasp. According to the American Optometric Association (AOA), newborns can see eight to ten inches from their faces. Young infants enjoy looking at faces, pets such as dogs and cats, and even their own hands. These objects are interesting as they come in and out of view. People's faces, in particular, capture babies' attention because they often react to the babies' movements, expressions, and vocalizations. They like handling cotton scarves and handkerchiefs that are small enough for the baby to lift and will not hurt if dropped. Other lightweight items, such as wicker balls, new bath poufs, and balled-up socks work well, as they are easy for babies to grasp and hold onto.

Five to Twelve Months: What Can I Do with It?

By about five months of age, the AOA indicates that infants are beginning to control their eye movements and their eye-body coordination. Babies five to twelve months of age enjoy exploring items that offer a variety of sizes, textures, scents, weights, temperatures, and colors. Over time, try offering items such as loofahs and sponges; pinecones; wooden, wicker, and metal bowls; glass paperweights or railroad insulators; ribbons and scarves; and beads and necklaces.

Twelve to Twenty-Four Months: What Else Can This Do?

By one year of age, children are typically walking and interested in their environments. They explore at every opportunity. Items such as pinecones, while familiar, may continue to be interesting as the child explores different sizes and figures out that his little fingers fit really well into the spaces. Seashells offer interesting textures, colors, shapes, and sizes. They may feel cold to the touch, and a child may even be able to hear the "ocean" when he lifts a shell to his ear. Copper pots and pans make great containers for other items and may even nest into each other. They offer beautiful color and shine and also make good drums. Plumbing parts, such as PVC fittings and pipes cut to six- and twelve-inch lengths, are fun to try to fit together in different combinations. Spiky items, such as hair curlers, offer interesting texture and are likely new to most children. Old CDs are shiny and can be stacked, and they fit nicely onto little fingertips. Beads, napkin rings, and bracelets are beautiful and easy to fit inside other objects.

Twenty-Four to Thirty-Six Months: What Can This Become?

According to the American Academy of Pediatrics (AAP), by the age of two years, children enjoy finding hidden objects and are beginning to engage in make-believe play. They will pretend that familiar objects, such as a TV remote, are something else, such as a cell phone. They might pretend to use the object, pointing a TV remote at a wall and shouting, "Commercial!" They may put PVC pipes together and pretend they are vacuuming. They may use seashells, beads, pinecones, wooden pieces, or hair curlers to pretend they are cooking, putting the items in a pot, bowl, or measuring cup.

They enjoy exploring ways items can fit together or inside other items. As they approach three years of age, they may fit PVC pipes together to create shapes. They may hide small items such as shells or beads inside purses or baskets. They may experiment with stacking items or putting items onto their fingers. They also enjoy sorting items. They may line up shells, pinecones, or wooden blocks by size from smallest to largest.

Afterword

We want our children to develop to their fullest potential. As Alison Gopnik, author of several books on child development, pointed out in a 2016 article she wrote for the *New York Times*, decades of child-development research has taught us that we need to trust children to guide us in how to teach them best. When we watch carefully, we learn that young children need interesting playthings that appeal to all their senses and allow them to explore the everyday tools that they see family members using.

This natural, inexpensive approach is much more educational than so-called educational toys because it appeals to the child's curiosity and it adapts to the child's changing abilities. For example, a six-month-old might grasp and mouth a pinecone, getting sensory feedback about its woody taste, prickly edges, and surprising lightness for its size. The same child at fourteen months might put the pinecone in a pot and stir it with a spoon, imitating her daddy cooking potatoes for dinner. At nineteen months, she might race to the window and use the pinecone to point to the other pinecones she sees under the tree in the backyard, showing that she now has a mental category for *pinecone* or "things that pile up under trees." At twenty-five months, she might group bigger and smaller pinecones together, a premath sorting skill. At twenty-eight months she might stack pinecones to create a bear cave, recalling a favorite story or creating a new narrative.

If we can learn to value these activities as scientific exploration, we will realize that we can allow children to learn. We don't have to lure them into it with flashy, noisy toys.

References and Recommended Reading and Viewing

American Academy of Pediatrics. 2009. Developmental Milestones. https://www.healthychildren.org/

American Optometric Association. 2016. Infant Vision: Birth to 24 Months of Age. http://www.aoa.org/patients-and-public/good-vision-throughout-life/childrens-vision/infant-vision-birth-to-24-months-of-age?sso=y

Brazelton, T. Berry. 1991. *Touchpoints: The Definitive Video Series on Parenting.* Videocassette. Boston, MA: Consumer Vision.

Carson, Rachel. 1965. *The Sense of Wonder.* New York: Harper and Row.

Cornell, Joseph. 2003. *Sharing Nature.* Nevada City, CA: Crystal Clarity.

Edwards, Carolyn, Lella Gandini, and George Forman, eds. 1998. *The Hundred Languages of Children: The Reggio Emilia Approach— Advanced Reflections.* 2nd ed. Westport, CT: Ablex.

Gandini, Lella. 1993. "Fundamentals of the Reggio Emilia Approach to Early Childhood Education." *Young Children* 49(1): 4–8.

Gerber, Magda. 1986. "Selecting Toys for Infants." *Educaring* 7(2). http://www.magdagerber.org/selecting-toys-for-infants---vol-vii-no-2-spring-1986.html

Goldschmied, Elinor, and Sonia Jackson. 1994. *People under Three: Young Children in Day Care.* New York: Routledge.

Gopnik, Alison. 2016. "What Babies Know About Physics and Foreign Languages." *New York Times,* July 30, Sunday Review/Opinion: SR4, http://www.nytimes.com/2016/07/31/opinion/sunday/what-babies-know-about-physics-and-foreign-languages.html?_r=0

Hughes, Anita, and Elinor Goldschmied. 1991. *I Don't Need Toys: A Film about Play in the First Two Years of Life.* Ipswich, Suffolk, UK: Concord Media.

Huleatt, Helen. n.d. "Heuristic Play." Community Playthings. http://www.communityplaythings.co.uk/learning-library/articles/heuristic-play

Huleatt, Helen. n.d. "Treasure Baskets." Community Playthings. http://www.communityplaythings.co.uk/learning-library/articles/treasure-baskets

International Play Association. 2010. "Declaration of the Child's Right to Play" Available at http://ipaworld.org/about-us/declaration/ipa-declaration-of-the-childs-right-to-play/

Jackson, Sonia. 2009. "Elinor Goldschmied: Pioneering Expert in the Care of Babies and Young Children." *The Guardian* (UK), June 11, https://www.theguardian.com/society/2009/jun/12/obituary-elinor-goldschmied

Jackson, Sonia, and Ruth Forbes. 2015. *People under Three: Play, Work, and Learning in a Childcare Setting.* 3rd ed. London: Routledge.

Jackson, Valerie. 2009. "Elinor Goldschmied: The Pioneer of Treasure Baskets, Heuristic Play and the Key Person System." *The Therapeutic Care Journal*, May 1. http://www.thetcj.org/early-years/elinor-goldschmied-pioneer-of-treasure-baskets-heuristic-play-and-the-key-person-system

Kable, Jenny. 2010. "Theory of Loose Parts." *Let the Children Play.* Play Outside, February 10. http://www.letthechildrenplay.net/2010/01/how-children-use-outdoor-play-spaces.html

Lally, Ronald. 2010. "School Readiness Begins in Infancy." *Phi Delta Kappan* 92(3): 17–21.

Marcus, Leonard. 2012. "Mitsumasa Anno." *Show Me a Story! Why Picture Books Matter.* Somerville, MA: Candlewick.

Nicholson, Simon. 1972. "The Theory of Loose Parts: An Important Principle for Design Methodology." *Studies in Design Education Craft and Technology* 4(2): 5–14.

Nicholson, Simon. 1971. "How NOT to Cheat Children: The Theory of Loose Parts." *Landscape Architecture* 62: 30–34.

Parlakian, Rebecca, and Claire Learner. 2008. "Your Baby's Development: Age-Based Tips from Birth to 36 Months." Zero to Three. https://www.zerotothree.org/resources/series/your-baby-s-development-age-based-tips-from-birth-to-36-months

Royal National Institute of Blind People. 2015. "Treasure Baskets." *Learning through Play in the Early Years*. London, UK: RNIB.

Sobel, David. 2016. *Nature Preschools and Forest Kindergartens: The Handbook for Outdoor Learning*. St. Paul, MN: Redleaf.

Index

Find more award-winning Infant and Toddler titles from

GryphonHouse

Award-Winning Publisher of
Early Childhood Resources

First Art for Toddlers and Twos
978-0-87659-399-8
Item #10017
$19.95

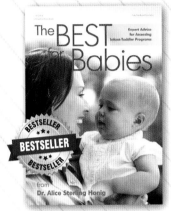

The Best for Babies
Expert Advice for Assessing
Infant-Toddler Programs
ISBN: 978-0-87659-554-1
Item #10704
$12.95

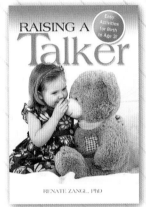

Raising a Talker
978-0-87659-473-5
Item #11505
$19.95

The Encyclopedia of Infant
and Toddler Activities
978-0-87659-013-3
Item #13614
$19.95

Time for a Story
Sharing Books with Infants and Toddlers
978-0-87659-657-9
Item #10058
$19.95

125 Brain Games for
Babies
978-0-87659-391-2
Item #13533
$16.95

125 Brain Games for
Toddlers and Twos
978-0-87659-392-9
Item #13534
$16.95